BASILE MOREAU

Blessed
BASILE MOREAU

FOUNDER OF THE CONGREGATIONS OF HOLY CROSS

FIDES

The photos in this book are taken from the Archives of the French Canadian Priests and the Museum of the Sisters of Holy Cross.

Catalogued before the publication of Library and Archives Canada

Main entry under title:

Basile Moreau, Founder of the Congregations of Holy Cross

Issued also in French under title: Basile Moreau; in Spanish under title: El beato Basilio Moreau; and in Portuguese under title: O bem-aventurado Basile Moreau.

ISBN 978-2-7621-2705-8

1. Moreau, Basile, 1799-1873. 2. Congregation of Holy Cross - History. 3. Catholic Church - Clergy - Biography. 4. Brothers (Religious) - France - Biography.

BX4705.M563B3713 2007   271'.79   C2007-940705-6

Legal deposit: third quarter, 2007
Bibliothèque et Archives nationales du Québec

© Éditions Fides, 2007

Éditions Fides acknowledges the financial support of the Government of Canada through the Book Publishing Industry Development Program (BPIDP) for their publishing activities. Éditions Fides also wishes to thank the Canadian Council for the Arts and the Société de développement des entreprises culturelles du Québec (SODEC). Éditions Fides is funded by the Government of Quebec tax program for publishing, a program managed by Sodec.

PRINTED IN CANADA IN JULY 2007

This book was prepared for the celebration
of the Beatification of Basile Moreau,
September 15, 2007, Le Mans, France

FOREWORD

Father Basile Moreau proclaimed Blessed

On April 28th last, Benedict XVI announced the forthcoming beatification of Father Basile Moreau. The beatification will take place in Le Mans, where Basile Moreau carried out his ministry as priest and founder of the religious family of Holy Cross, and where he died.

Born in 1799 in Laigné-en-Belin, young Basile was very soon noticed by the parish priest for his piety and enthusiasm. After completing his studies at Château-Gontier and in Le Mans, he was ordained priest in 1821 at the Church of the Visitation (Place de la République). For thirteen years, he dedicated himself wholeheartedly to the ministry of teaching and spiritual accompaniment of seminarians entrusted to him. At the same time his gifts as a preacher did not go unnoticed. Parish priests of the diocese called upon him to bring the Word of God to their parishioners.

The bishops appealed to his qualities as an organizer. In 1833, Bishop Carron put him in charge of founding a shelter for girls in difficulty. Together with the religious women of Our Lady of Charity he founded the Bon Pasteur Home, where he remained as ecclesiastical superior for twenty-five years. In 1835, Bishop Bouvier asked him to form a group of diocesan missionaries and he also entrusted him with the Institute of the Brothers of St Joseph, founded by Father Dujarié in Ruillé-sur-Loir. Father Moreau brought priests and brothers together in the Holy Cross Parish in Le Mans. He added a group of sisters to them and thus became the founder of the Holy Cross religious family (1840). In 1857, Rome approved the "Congregation of Holy Cross" (priests and brothers) and ten years later, the "Congregation of the Marianite Sisters".

A talented educator and pioneer of education in La Sarthe, Father Moreau opened the first secondary school at Holy Cross. (It would later be taken over by the Jesuits; later still the chapel would become the parish church, Our Lady of Holy Cross.) The renown of Holy Cross spread beyond the diocese. Many charitable works and institutions, especially schools and boarding schools, appeared in several regions of France. At the request of the bishops, Father Moreau sent priests and brothers to Algeria, followed by groups of religious men and women to the United States of America, Canada, and Bengal. The Pope asked him to open an orphanage in Rome. Basile Moreau's apostolic dynamism and determination impressed everyone. There was no lack of praise for him, nor of opposition and adversity of all kinds. He resigned as Superior General in 1866, and was disowned and abandoned. However, he continued to preach and to be of service to parish priests right up to his death on January 20, 1873.

After a long period of silence, a return to the founder begun ... With the support of Cardinal Grente, the Cause for his beatification was presented in Rome in 1955. Pope John Paul II declared him Venerable in 2003, and Benedict XVI has announced his beatification in 2007.

† Jacques FAIVRE
Bishop of Le Mans

I

BASILE MOREAU
PRIEST OF THE DIOCESE OF LE MANS
FOUNDER OF THE RELIGIOUS FAMILY
OF HOLY CROSS

P. Jean Proust, c.s.c.

Basile Moreau – A Man from La Sarthe

Basile Moreau was born in Laigné-en-Belin in the neighbourhood of Haut-Éclair. His parents cultivated a small plot of land and raised a few farm animals in order to provide for their fourteen children. His father also had a small wine business; he kept his casks in a wine cellar that can still be seen today. In the nearby church there is a memorial plaque commemorating Basile's baptism, and several stained glass windows bear witness to the superior of Holy Cross' attachment to the parish of his birth.

After three years at the seminary college of Château-Gontier, followed by four years at the seminaries of Le Mans, Basile was ordained to the priesthood at the age of twenty-two. After ordination, his bishop sent him to Paris to complete his formation with the Sulpicians. He returned to Le Mans in 1823 and remained there, leaving only to preach in neighbouring villages, to visit his religious family, or to make an occasional trip to Rome on behalf of his congregation.

It is easy to evoke the memory of Father Moreau in many areas of Le Mans, the first place being, naturally, the Church of Notre-Dame de Sainte-Croix (Our

Baptismal font of the church in Laigné-en-Belin.

Basile began his studies in the rectory of Laigné-en-Belin.

Birthplace of Basile Moreau in Laigné-en-Belin, Sarthe, France.

Lady of Holy Cross), which was the church of his religious family and the chapel of the school he established (today known as the Mangin Barracks) where the sons of the families of Le Mans and La Sarthe were sent to study. The crypt of the church contains the tomb of the Founder. The recumbent figure is the work of sculptor Henri Charlier.

Not far from the church, there is an enclosure in the Holy Cross Cemetery reserved for the deceased members of the community. Before being transferred to the church of Notre-Dame de Sainte-Croix, Father Moreau's body was buried in the little chapel that is now the resting place of Mother Mary of the Seven Dolors, the first superior of the Marianite Sisters.

Father Moreau established the novitiate for the priests atop the hill of Gazonfier. He called the novitiate "La Solitude". It is now a retirement home for the Marianite Sisters. The Brothers' novitiate was built further away in the country, at a place called La Charbonnière.

On another hill in the town, in the old Abbey of St. Vincent, (today Lycée Bellevue), stood St. Vincent Theological Seminary, where Basile Moreau studied,

This house, occupied by Holy Cross since 1840 and named Solitude of the Saviour, was the first novitiate of the Holy Cross priests. It forms the central part of the present residence of the Marianites of Holy Cross at 35, rue de la Solitude.

and later taught Scripture and dogma. It was there, as assistant superior, that he gathered together a number of young priests, some of whom would later become the first Holy Cross priests.

The philosophy seminary was located in the former Hôtel de Tessé. Basile Moreau was also a frequent visitor at the episcopal palace of Tessé built by Bishop Bouvier, which is now the Museum of Fine Arts.

Basile was ordained sub-deacon in St Julien's Cathedral. As assistant superior of the seminary and as an honorary canon of the cathedral, he often passed through one or another of the cathedral's portals to celebrate early morning

Mass, or to take part in a pontifical office, or quite simply just to sit and spend some time in meditation. A good number of Holy Cross priests were ordained in that very cathedral, both in his day and in ours.

Facing the cathedral's Roman portal, on the corner by the Hôtel du Grabatoire, which is now the bishop's residence, the Pans de Gorron open out, leading down to the quays. Father Moreau often went down these steep steps to reach the Convent of the Good Shepherd, where he was the ecclesiastical superior for twenty-five years. It was there, in the Convent of the Good Shepherd, that the first Marianite Sisters were formed for religious life.

Basile Moreau was ordained priest in 1821, in the Chapel of the Visitation, which bordered the former market square (now Place de la République). It was from this square, surrounded by inns and taverns, that the stage-coaches and other public conveyances would leave for various destinations.

On several occasions, Father Moreau preached at the churches of Notre-Dame de la Couture, Notre-Dame du Pré, Saint-Benoit, and Saint Martin de Pontlieue. He also preached at the Carmelite convent in the small village of Butte and at the convent of the Visitation Sisters, near the present-day Centre de l'Etoile... Lastly, a few kilometres from Le Mans, there is the ancient church of Yvré-l'Evêque, where he celebrated his last Mass.

For fifty-four years, Basile Moreau shared the lives of the people of Le Mans. He was on good terms with the people in the neighbourhood, the parents of the students, the Associates of the Good Shepherd and St. Joseph, his benefactors, the town authorities, and the workmen for whom he found employment. The Bollée Foundry was close to Notre-Dame de Sainte-Croix. Three Bollée bells rang out to announce the consecration of the Church of Notre-Dame (Later, a set of twenty-four bells was sent to the University of Notre Dame in Indiana). Water was distributed throughout the school thanks to the Bollée hydraulic rams.

The contemporary journalist, Louis Veuillot, described Father Moreau in May 1846:

At first he seems like one of those country priests from whom you do not expect very much, and whose appearance is in no way belied by his Le Mans accent, which pares down even further his great simplicity of speech... After speaking with him for a while, you notice that he has discerning eyes, that his mind is direct, firm and fertile, and that his heart is consumed with love. He is a great man and a saint.

Basile Moreau – A Man of the 19th Century

B asile Moreau was born on February 11, 1799, or rather, on the 23rd day of the fifth month of the year VII of the French Republican calendar. France had barely emerged from the Great Revolution. The memory of those ten terrible years would haunt people's minds for a long time to come. In 1834, Father Moreau recalled in a sermon:

> Have you forgotten that sad spectacle of a population run mad in the throes of its sacrilegious rage, destroying crosses, pillaging places of worship, desecrating sacred vessels, smashing tabernacles, and crying death to the clergy? It is true that ever since that appalling upheaval at the end of the last century, there has been some degree of a return to order and a move towards religion is emerging almost everywhere; but in the midst of society's painful labour, which should undoubtedly produce some triumphs for the faith, how many crimes and abominations of all kinds there have been!

It took some time for the political situation in France to stabilize. From the time of Basile Moreau's birth in 1799 to his death in 1873, about ten different

political regimes succeeded each other: the Consulate, the First Empire, the Restoration with Louis XVIII and Charles X, the July Monarchy with Louis-Philippe, the Second Republic, the Second Empire, the Third Republic. The people followed along as best they could, and so did the church. Whereas the Republicans were inclined to be anti-clerical, the majority of Catholics remained Monarchists. Traditionally, Father Moreau was a Legitimist:

I mourn the passing of that ancient and long respected rule, upon which the stability of public order used to rest, the remains of which have become a vast inheritance fought over by greedy heirs with weapons in their hands ... I feel the need to forewarn you against this false and seductive view of the sovereignty of the people that drives them to rise up against any authority that they have not themselves established, or at least recognized and accepted, because it is that which has been troubling people's minds and turning our country turbulent for the past sixty years ... (*Circular Letter,* December 8, 1851)

However, he was on occasion capable of professing political neutrality. At the inauguration of a Brothers' school in 1845, he declared:

One of the benefits of the July Revolution was the proclamation of freedom of worship and primary education. I now profess to hold no political opinion. All I see in the different parties are brothers in turmoil; I am neither Republican, nor Liberal, nor Legitimist: I am a priest and no more. My Brothers cannot hold a contrary opinion on this issue and remain a part of my congregation. Our motto is: Union, charity, obedience to the civil authorities and the law; our flag: the bare cross.

During a retreat at the Trappist Monastery of Soligny in 1847, he met the King, Louis-Philippe. He thanked the King for the 1843 decree enabling the Holy Cross Brothers to teach in Algerian schools. Then, without any hesitation, he proceeded to describe to the King all the interests of the Congregation. The list of personalities – mayors, school inspectors, government prefects, representatives of the people, state councillors, ministers – with whom he had entered into contact, or conflict, when he had had to defend the interests of his various schools, was long:

Though I may not believe in privileges or special favours, neither do I care to be deprived of the benefit of the law without good reason. As a priest, I have a duty to do all I can for religion so as to extend its influence. As the French superior of a teaching body, it is my duty to do all that is in my power to contribute to the good education of the youth and thus contribute to the well-being of my country.

He never hesitated to lock horns with the authorities when they overstepped their rights. And he could be quite tenacious! One of the prefects of Le Mans wrote to the Minister of Education that Father Moreau was the kind of person who, when shown the door, would come right back in again through the window!

The 19th century, a century of political revolutions, also saw the birth of the first industrial revolution, the revolution of coal, steam, and steel. In Le Mans, Father Moreau witnessed the social evolution that was brought about in its wake. Although the province of La Sarthe remained essentially agricultural, the towns, especially after the arrival of the railway in 1854, built up new industries. As a result, the lives of the inhabitants underwent a profound change. With his rural background, Father Moreau understood and loved labourers. He frequently visited the building site of his church during its construction and would gather the workers for meals over which he presided, and spoke to them as though they were his helpers in the building of the house of God.

In 1848, some political fanatics wanted to set fire to the community buildings in Sainte-Croix, on the pretext that cloth was being made there to be sold so cheaply as to take the bread out of the weavers' mouths. Father Moreau approached these men and managed to convince them to place the house under their protection!

A friend of Frederick Ozanam, Father Moreau established a St Vincent de Paul Society in the school in 1844. On their days off, the pupils would visit poor families and take them food, clothing, and medicine. In times of need, he organized the distribution of food. In 1846, when the districts on the right bank of the river were submerged under water, he himself went out in a boat to bring help to the victims. When cholera raged in the unhealthy parts of the town in 1849, he offered the authorities the services of the Brothers as nurses and opened the house at La Charbonnière to receive the sick. As for the Marianite Sisters, they went from house to house in the town to care for the sick in their own homes.

Basile Moreau – A Priest of Le Mans

Father Moreau and the Bishops of Le Mans

Basile received tonsure and minor orders from Bishop de Pidoll. Bishop de La Myre conferred the orders of sub-deacon and deacon and ordained him to the priesthood; he also sent him to the Sulpicians to prepare for the teaching profession. Bishop Carron entrusted the young priest with important missions: the launching of a fund-raising drive to support the Christian Brothers' schools, the setting up of a pension fund for elderly and infirm priests, and the establishment of the Home of Our Lady of Charity for young delinquent girls and girls in difficulty.

Bishop Bouvier, who was bishop from 1834 to 1855, valued Father Moreau's efforts in the seminary. In 1835, he asked him to take over the direction of the Brothers of St. Joseph and to establish a group of diocesan missionaries. On August 15, 1840, the bishop received his religious profession of vows; on October 18th of the same year, he blessed the novitiate of priests at La Solitude, and, on March 18, 1842, he blessed the cornerstone of the church. However, he vigorously opposed Father Moreau's other projects: a society of priests for teaching, a secondary boarding school at Sainte-Croix, a community of religious women. Right up to his death he intervened with Rome to prevent the Congregation of Holy Cross from being recognized as a congregation of pontifical right.

Bishop Nanquette, on the contrary, made it quite clear that his sympathies lay with Father Moreau. He intervened with Rome in favour of the Congregation of Holy Cross. Together with Cardinal Donnet and eight other bishops he attended the ceremony for the consecration of the church on June 17, 1857. Bishop Fillion, however, joined the ranks of his opponents, admitting all the while that Basile Moreau might be canonized one day!

Basile Moreau - Seminary Director (1823 – 1836)

After the revolutionary period, which saw the disappearance of two-thirds of the priests in France, and the Empire's wars, which decimated the ranks of those of an age to become seminarians, the diocese of Le Mans,

Father Moreau had the statue of Our Lady of the Solitude erected near the Solitude of the Saviour where he often withdrew to pray and reflect on the Constitutions and Statutes of the Congregation of Holy Cross.

like many other French dioceses, experienced a great shortage of priests. To foster vocations and help them flourish, the bishops encouraged pre-seminary schools in parishes much like the one run by Mr. Le Provost at Laigné when Basile Moreau was a youth, and they established minor seminaries (like the school at Château-Gontier) and major seminaries (Tessé and St Vincent). In 1821, forty-two priests were ordained (including Basile Moreau); by 1830, there were sixty-eight ordinations.

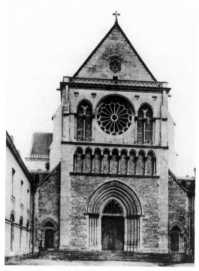

The building of the church of Notre-Dame-de-Sainte-Croix took from 1840 to 1856. The church was consecrated on June 17, 1857.

In 1818, while superior of St. Vincent Seminary, Mgr Bouvier endeavoured to raise the seminary's educational standard; he developed a course in theology that was used in sixty dioceses. Basile Moreau also had the training of the seminarians very much at heart. Already in 1822, while a student in Paris, he suggested to the superior of the seminary at Tessé that he be more demanding with respect to discipline and study. In 1828, he expressed a desire for better training of priests who were also to be teachers. In his eagerness to renew teaching he adopted and spread the liberal ideas of Lamennais; but when Rome censured the author of *Paroles d'un*

Croyant (Words of a Believer), he publicly expressed his regret at having succumbed to such youthful folly. When he became the seminary's assistant superior in 1834, he showed what an innovator he was by introducing a physical science course in the seminary.

Like many bishops of the time, Bishop Bouvier tended towards Gallicanism. Finding Basile Moreau too Ultramontanist in his teachings on the Church, he transferred him to the chair of Holy Scripture. Father Moreau always remained a member of the Roman party along with his friends Heurtebize, Lottin, Piolin, Guillois ... and Dom Guéranger. Despite the opposition of the bishop of Le Mans, he adopted the Roman liturgical forms for Holy Cross, and used all means available to obtain Roman approbation for his congregation.

The Master and his Disciples

Father Moreau was the spiritual director for a large number of seminarians and young priests. Several of them joined the Auxiliary Priests and some even made their religious profession. It came to such a point that the bishop became concerned at seeing his best priests joining Holy Cross. Many of them had strong personalities, which they showed much later. Recognizing their abilities, Father Moreau made them his closest associates in the government of his congregation. Others were Holy Cross pioneers in Algeria, the United States, Canada, and Bengal. No history of the origins of Holy Cross can pass over in silence such names as Pierre Chappé of Brûlon, Augustin Saunier of Pontlieue, Édouard Sorin of Ahuillé, Louis Champeau of Breil, Victor Drouelle of Conlie, Joseph Rézé of Sablé, and Louis Vérité of Montfort-le-Rotrou.

Friends and Foes

Some priests in the diocese, including the principal of the school in Le Mans, a seminary bursar, and a vicar general opposed Father Moreau's activities. However, his friends far outnumbered them: Robert Jobbé de Lisle, who donated the property of Notre-Dame; Julien Clocheau and Louis Joubert, members the civil society of Holy Cross; Pierre Dubignon, who appointed him his sole heir; Louis-Jean Fillion, who ended his days at Notre-Dame-de-Sainte-Croix; and Benjamin Heurtebize, who Father Moreau appointed novice master in 1840, and who spoke out on his behalf on several occasions. The parish priests of Notre-Dame de la Couture (Mr. Huard), Notre-Dame-du-Pré (Mr. Guillot and Mr. Livet), and Saint Benoit (Mr. Le Baillif), were also friends, as well as Mr. René Métivier, parish priest of Yvré-l'Eveque, where he celebrated his last Mass. There were even more friends: Magloire Tournesac, who drew up the plans for school and church before joining the Jesuits, Prosper Guéranger, Abbot of Solesmes, and many others.

Basile Moreau – A Founder

In his youth, Basile Moreau dreamed of becoming a missionary in distant lands or of the solitary life in a Trappist monastery. However, obedience kept him in a seminary for thirteen years. Once in contact with real everyday life, his dreams were transformed into projects, and he devoted the rest of his life to bringing them to completion.

As a young priest in Paris, a parish mission sparked in him a desire to evangelize the de-christianized countryside. On his return to Le Mans, he contacted Father Dujarié, who was at this time was trying to form a group of preachers. The plan did not bear fruit; it was only put off until a later time.

As assistant superior of the seminary in Le Mans, he wanted a better training for priests in order to raise the standard of teaching in schools and seminaries. At his own expense, he sent young priests from Le Mans to study at the Sorbonne. It was a marvellous gesture on his part, one that was destined to have no future.

In 1835 the bishop encouraged him to form a team of diocesan missionaries. He contacted two priests and two seminarians. Together, in the middle of the summer, in the silence of the Trappist monastery of Port-du-Salut, they drew up

Father Jacques François Dujarié (1767-1838), founder of the Brothers of Saint Joseph. In 1806, Father Dujarié, pastor of Ruillé, founded a community of Sisters of Providence. Fourteen years later, he began an Institute of Brothers for the education of the youth in the rural areas. In August 1835, Father Dujarié entrusted the Brothers of Saint Joseph to Father Moreau.

Mother Mary of Seven Dolors, Father Moreau's collaborator in the foundation of the Marianites of Holy Cross.

their plans. In the autumn they were joined by some companions at St Vincent's Seminary. In January of the following year, they took the name of "Auxiliary Priests" and began to preach in parishes.

That same year, the bishop asked Father Moreau to assume the direction of the Brothers of St. Joseph, founded fifteen years earlier in Ruillé by Father Dujarié. He knew them already, having preached their retreats. One of them, André Mottais, had begged him to come to their assistance. The matter was settled on August 31st. On All Saints' Day of that year, he transferred the Brothers' novitiate to the commune of Sainte-Croix, where the property of Notre-Dame had been placed at his disposal.

At the beginning of school term in 1836, having left the seminary, he looked around for accommodation for the Auxiliary Priests. He rented a house close to Notre-Dame. On March 1st, 1837, he had both brothers and priests sign a pact of union and gave them a common mission: to educate the youth and evangelize the countryside.

He enlisted the help of some women for the domestic services of the community and the boarding school; these were the first sisters. On January 1, 1840, he revealed a new project: to associate the sisters with the brothers and priests. He proposed religious vows for them all. He himself made his religious profession on August 15th. Eight days later (despite opposition from the bishop), he gathered everyone together in a Chapter: the Association of Holy Cross was born.

On August 4, 1841, the woman who would one day become the superior of the Marianites, Mother Mary of the Seven Dolors, arrived at Holy Cross. On September 1st the Rector of the Association published a circular letter: the Charter of Holy Cross. Henceforth the three societies would form a single family and there would be effective apostolic collaboration among them. Father Moreau even foresaw this audacious project approved by Rome! Was this only a dream?

In order to respond to numerous requests from bishops, the Association assumed an international dimension. By 1840, two priests and six brothers were working in Algeria. The following year, six brothers and a priest were sent to the United States of America. They were joined later by four sisters in 1843. In 1847, a group of fourteen missionaries, priests, brothers, and sisters arrived in Canada. Pope Pius IX intervened in 1850 by placing an orphanage in Rome in the care of Holy Cross, and two years later he entrusted the Bengal Mission to Holy Cross. The "distant lands" that Father had dreamed of were to be evangelized by his sons and daughters.

Bishop Bouvier did not look kindly upon the expansion that was taking priests and other co-workers from his diocese. However, this missionary apostolate was helping to gain favor from Rome. On May 13, 1857, the pope approved the Congregation of Holy Cross, at least, the priests and brothers. It would be another ten years before the Marianite Sisters were approved. The Founder's dream had not fully been realized, but he accepted the restriction because the pope had decided upon it.

A great thanksgiving celebration was held in the Church of Notre-Dame de Sainte-Croix June 18, 1857, the day of its consecration, in the presence of a cardinal; nine bishops (including Bishop Nanquette of Le Mans); the Abbot of Solesmes, who was accompanied by a group of monks who provided the Gregorian chant; and municipal and departmental authorities.

Dreams and projects; opposition and unexpected interventions; so many difficulties and worries; the founding of Holy Cross was a veritable saga! Father Moreau would say that it was "the work of God".

If I could have foreseen the developments of the Congregation of Holy Cross from the outset, I could have regulated and coordinated everything in advance. If such were the case, however, this Congregation would have been a merely human combination and not the work of divine Providence. The fact of the matter is that it began and developed in a manner so mysterious, that I can claim for myself neither credit for its foundation nor merit for its progress. Therein lies the indubitable proof that God alone is its author, since according to St. Augustine, "when we cannot find the cause of a good work, we must recognize that the Lord is its beginning and author". (*Circular Letter*, April 13, 1858).

Basile Moreau – A Man of Action

Father Moreau was one of the builders of Catholic renewal in 19th-century France. With his ardent and enterprising nature, he set about this immense undertaking in various sectors, not least of which was the training of priests, a task to which he obediently devoted thirteen years of his life, throwing himself into it with all his heart and mind.

At the same time, in his passion for the Word of God, he preached in the various parishes of the diocese, and everywhere else he was asked to do so. His talent as a speaker and the power of his conviction attracted large audiences and led to many conversions. Between 1836 and 1847, the Auxiliary Priests formed by him for this ministry, preached numerous retreats, missions, and Advent and Lenten services throughout the diocese of Le Mans and in neighbouring dioceses. Their superior often accompanied them, always giving the opening and closing sermons himself. A circular letter written from Javron, dated January 10, 1843, illustrates the pace at which he worked: "... a parish in the department of Mayenne, where, with three of my fellow-priests, I am giving a mission. I shall finish this mission just in time to give another at Montfort and one at Pont-de-Gennes,

Stained-glass windows situated in the church of Notre-Dame-de-Sainte-Croix.

some leagues from Le Mans, after opening the mission at Viré near Brûlon. Then I am to give another mission at Bouère, in addition to the retreat which I have promised to the college of Château-Gontier."

When the nave of the church of Notre-Dame de Sainte-Croix was opened to the faithful in 1847, people came from all over town to listen to Father Moreau, who preached there every Sunday for as long as he was able. In his last years, he returned to his ministry as an Auxiliary Priest — that is, as a preacher. Between 1867 and 1872, he preached in more than fifty parishes. The retreats and missions often lasted three weeks at a time: one for women, one for men, and one for young people. In 1867, he wrote as follows to his sister Josephine: "Yesterday I spoke to the women at 6:30 a.m., to the men at 8:15 a.m., and to both at 10.30 a.m.; then to the women at 2:00 p.m., the men at 4:00 p.m. and to everyone together at 6.30 pm., for almost an hour each time, and the church was always full. I am told that I look very tired, but unless I lose my voice, I shall start another mission this very evening." It was while preaching at Yvré-l'Evêque on January 1, 1873, that he fell ill, never to recover.

As Father Dujarié's successor in the direction of the Brothers of St. Joseph, Father Moreau took an active part in the Christian education of children and young people, one of the most pressing needs of the time. From the very beginning, he was demanding concerning the training of the brothers. He reminded them of the importance of their mission: "The children who attend your school today are the men of the future and the fathers of the generations to come." For Father Moreau, Christian education was a work of resurrection and an option for the future. The direction of the brothers and the defense of schools were to be among his greatest concerns.

He showed the same zeal towards the development of the Collège Sainte-Croix. A true forerunner in the battle for the freedom of secondary education, he stood firm in the face of opposition, whether it came from the civil authorities or the bishop. He initiated the introduction of Latin and Greek in the boarding school, and opened up secondary level classes to everyone up to the level of philosophy. The Minister for Public Education, Mr. de Falloux, gave him this privilege during a personal interview on January 12, 1849, a year before it became law. For Father Moreau, "full exercise" was indispensable:

> To prepare youth with all its lights and virtues to come to the aid of modern society, a society moulded by revolutions, in addition to inculcating the law of duty and the principles of faith, we must provide the child's intelligence with all the instruction needed to pursue the different careers he may be called upon to follow. (*Etrennes Spirituelles*, 1850)

Nevertheless, true to his evangelical spirit, Father Moreau never forgot "service to the poor." The purpose of the Congregation of the Priests and Brothers, as stated in the first Constitution, was: " ... preaching the divine word in the countryside and in foreign missions ... and the instruction and education of youth, with a particular care for poor and abandoned children," and that of the Sisters was: " ... to instruct youth and provide a Christian upbringing, by founding, either in France and its colonies or abroad, not only primary schools but also boarding schools, workshops, and homes, etc., in particular for poor and abandoned children." In fact, the first task undertaken by Holy Cross outside of France was to help orphans in Algeria. Similar institutions followed in Indiana, New Orleans, Rome, Poland, and Bengal.

Father Moreau, who in the springtime of his priesthood had dreamed of foreign missionary work, was never indifferent to the requests he received from all over the world. When the Holy See suggested the Bengal mission, he accepted at once. It did not matter whether he had the people or the resources. He trusted in Providence.

I have been blamed by some for accepting this mission, on the grounds that all the other congregations had refused it and that no good can be done there. To this criticism I have replied, as in similar circumstances I shall always reply, that my principle with regard to foundations is neither to ask nor to refuse anything, when all indications seem to point to a plan of Providence. (*Circular, Letter* January 1, 1858)

Basile Moreau – A Man of God

When choosing the name of one of the founders of Eastern monasticism, and the name of a father of the desert, Father Moreau's parents could not have foreseen that their child would one day himself be a man of great austerity, intense inner life, and the founder of a religious family. It was not in their choice of Christian names that his parents helped him discover his path and prepared him for his mission, but it was through the education they gave him. Together with the joy of living in a united family, Basile Anthony learned from them a sense of duty and work, as well as the need to live one's faith with courage.

There were other examples of fidelity and courage that marked his youth, particularly the examples of the priests around him, or those he had heard about. During the Reign of Terror, the parish priest of Laigné, Mr. Renaudin, died in prison in Le Mans, his curate, Mr. Robin, was deported to Spain, Mr. Le Provost, who taught Basile his catechism and a bit of Latin, exercised his ministry in secret like Jacques Dujarié. The superior of the Collège Château-Gontier, Mr. Horeau, also spent two years in prison. The good Father Fillion, his spiritual father, was his friend and confidant for forty years.

The years in the seminary also contributed to providing a solid basis for the inner life of the young Basile, who, it was noted, had a tendency to go beyond what was asked of him. He was already striving to put into practice the spirit of the evangelical counsels. Before becoming a sub-deacon, he privately made the three vows of poverty, chastity, and obedience, to which he added the vow of mortification. Two years later he resolved " ... to be faithful to my own special rule and combine this sacrifice with the sacrifice of Our Lord, to become accustomed to receiving as coming from God all that might trouble and upset me." He was already burning with zeal. The morning after his first Mass, he informed his bishop of his longing to work in the foreign missions and later, he confided to Father Fillion how much he would like to evangelize the countryside.

Bishop de La Myre, however, wanted him to become a seminary professor and sent him to Paris to complete his formation with the Sulpicians. During his two years there, the young priest was imbued with the French school of spirituality, and under the firm direction of Mr. Mollevaut, he learned the practice of humility, gentleness and moderation. For over twenty-five years Mr. Mollevaut was his advisor in all important matters. After returning to Le Mans, Basile Moreau taught at the seminary. His study of philosophy provided him with the maturity of spirit he would need for his future foundations; his study of theology provided him with a sound doctrinal basis for his preaching and his study of Holy Scripture added zest to his spiritual teaching.

When he left the seminary in the autumn of 1836 to devote himself totally to the work of Holy Cross, his spirituality took on a more apostolic nature. Being a man of determination and of action, he felt himself in harmony with Ignatius of Loyola, who, like him, was involved in the apostolate and government of religious communities. However, he was still very much attracted by the silence and austerity of the Trappists, and under the influence of Solesmes, his piety took on a liturgical tone.

It was Father Moreau's life that best revealed his spirituality. He was a man of great faith and he had an absolute trust in Providence. He desired passionately to imitate Christ in all His mysteries. He had a burning zeal and was totally disposed to undertake anything in the service of the Church and of society. He did not write long tracts. His spiritual teaching emerged according to circumstances, in his *Sermons, Circular Letters, Catechism of the Christian and Religious Life, Christian Meditations, Books of Rules, Directories,* and his book on *Christian Education.*

What he sought with all his heart to impress upon the members of his religious family was the "spirit of union." He desired this union not only because every religious congregation should imitate the early Christians who had but "one heart" and "one soul," but also because he had to face the challenge of enabling three communities to live together. He wanted his congregation to be one united family, like the Holy Family of Nazareth. He did not propose that they imitate the hidden life of Nazareth, but rather that they imitate the charity that united its three members, Jesus, Mary, and Joseph.

> Above all, let us work with that strength, unity and clear understanding which come from the mutual cooperation and the possession of all things in common. We must never lose sight of the fact that strength of members, joined with unity of aim and action, is the greatest of all strengths and is limited only by the bonds of the possible. Besides, it is this perfect unity which, with the aid of grace, I have tried to cement among the various members of our association by consecrating the priests to the Sacred Heart of Jesus, the brothers to the Most Pure Heart of St. Joseph, and the sisters to the Immaculate Heart of Mary. Thus these three establishments, although separated by special dwelling places and special rules, will be united among themselves like the Holy Family... (*Circular Letter*, January 5, 1844)

The 19th century was a Marian century. Father Moreau was deeply devoted to the Virgin Mary, to whom his parents had consecrated him. On the day of his religious profession, he added the name Mary to his Christian names. He appointed himself apostle of the month of Mary at the seminary in Le Mans and at Holy Cross. His Marian devotion was expressed in a very special way towards the mystery of the Virgin's compassion. He placed his religious family under the patronage of Our Lady of Holy Cross.

Basile Moreau – A Man of the Cross

Holy Cross was the name of the place where the congregation was born, but it is possible that the name was providential. The mystery of the Cross met with a deep and powerful response in the soul of Father Moreau. He undoubtedly used that name to underline the importance of the cross in one's spiritual life, and he gave as a motto to his community the liturgical verse: *Hail, O Cross, our only hope.*

Father Moreau wrote of the mystery of the cross in his early circular letters. Describing the difficulties encountered in his different missions, he said:

> The tree of the cross has been planted where our worthy religious dwell! At times, its roots are the fewness of members and lack of funds; at others, sickness and contradictions. But these religious have learned to savor its life-giving fruits, and if God in His goodness preserves them in the admirable dispositions which they have shown thus far, they will never taste death, for the fruits of the cross are the same as those of the tree of life which was planted in the Garden of Paradise. But this fruit is bitter for a time, and how few there are who wish to feed on it! Consequently, how few there are who enjoy true life! It is my fond hope that all of you who have

so generously offered yourselves for these far-away missions are already filled with this life. In order to be a foreign missionary, one must know the mystery of the cross... Try, then to become perfect copies of the divine model, and nothing will ever shake your vocation. Not only will you carry whatever crosses you encounter in accomplishing the duties of your holy state, but you will love these crosses. Yes, you will even desire them and, after the example of our Lord, will choose them in preference to everything else. (*Circular Letter,* January 8, 1841)

There are, doubtless, a goodly number of crosses for one year, not to mention those which from time to time are provided by ill-will, lying and slander. Far from complaining of these trials, we must learn to love them, for if we bear them as we should they are worth their weight in gold. These nails and thorns will be changed later into the many precious stones which will make up the crown of glory reserved for those who have been faithful to the duties of their vocation and have worn lovingly, even to the end, their Savior's crown of thorns. (*Circular Letter*, January 4, 1845

Later, the trials and tribulations of the Founder became steadily more and more painful. Father Sorin's refusal to assume responsibility for the Bengal Mission was like a blow to his heart, as were his threats to break away. In the autumn of 1855, overwhelmed by financial problems and slander, he foresaw the ruin of his congregation. Feeling responsible, he underwent a time of great inner trial, a veritable night of the spirit.

At that moment I understood something of Our Lord's feeling of abandonment in his agony, as he went from his father to his disciples without finding any consolation. I then understood perfectly Judas' suicide, and it would have been a great favor if only someone could have removed the two objects that I had acquired which were lying on top of my desk. One was a passport to go abroad that I had requested from the Ministry of Foreign Affairs, and the other five hundred francs to pay for my trip; because I would have certainly yielded to the temptation had I not kept my eyes fixed on my crucifix all the time. I gazed upon it for days at a time.

Two years later, his congregation was approved by Rome and his church was consecrated: for Father Moreau, it was Mount Tabor after the Agony. But, very soon afterwards, he resumed his Calvary. The extortions of a bursar placed the Paris house in bankruptcy and threatened the very existence of the congregation. The opposition of a group of faithful became more open, and complaints and accusations both to his bishop and even to Rome multiplied. Summoned to Rome to confront his accusers, he decided not to speak in his defense, like Christ during His Passion: "I shall go, but after I have heard the accusations of my companions I shall withdraw in silence and give up once and for all this administration that has brought me so much opposition."

He began offering his resignation from 1860 onwards. The announcement that it had been accepted by the pope reached him on June 14, 1866, his feast day! From that moment on, he had to carry his cross for a long time. He found himself utterly alone, pushed into the background by every possible means. Condemned by the General Chapter of 1868, he was stripped of everything. The motherhouse, his secondary school, the two novitiates, and his church were all put up for sale. In April 1869, with only the possessions left to him, he found shelter with his two sisters in their small house. Since the congregation was unable to provide him with any means of support, the Marianites brought him food. He defended himself against the deluge of insults and lies without any bitterness or hate, much in the same manner as Christ, who forgave his executioners: "I forgive them all and pray God to have pity on the debris of our congregation." He continued his ministry as an Auxiliary Priest to the very last hours of his life.

In 1867, Father Moreau drew up his spiritual testament. In 1871, he affirmed that his feelings towards his people had not changed.

I forgive with all my heart those who have wronged me either by damaging my reputation or the assets in my care, and respectfully beg Divine Mercy, through the intercession of the Blessed Virgin and St Joseph, to forgive them and I bless God for having found me worthy enough to suffer in working for His glory.

Statue placed in the garden of the
Marianites' Residence. Note the tree, a symbol
of the three branches of Holy Cross, priests,
brothers, and sisters.

The Abbey of the Trappist monastery of Mortagne,
Father Moreau's favourite place for retreat and solitude.

It is in St. Julien Cathedral in Le Mans that Basile Moreau
was ordained subdeacon on May 27, 1820.

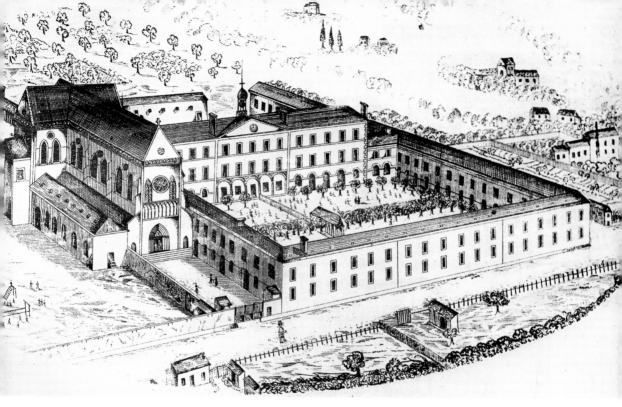

The complex of Notre-Dame-de-Sainte-Croix, built between 1838 and 1856, included an institution for education and a church. The Institution was under the direction of Holy Cross until 1869. The building is now known as Caserne Mangin. The church, formerly the college chapel, became the parish church of Notre-Dame-de-Sainte-Croix in 1938.

The church of Notre-Dame-de-Sainte-Croix –
Stained-glass windows are found
in the ambulatory behind the sanctuary.

R.M. AUGUSTA INDIANA 1843 TRMM DES SEPT DOULEURS RMMe DE St JULIEN CANADA 1847

Ste JULIE SUPÉRIEURE GÉNÉRALE FONDATRICE R.M. MARIE DE I St MATHIEU

1841

TOUT LA REGLE EST UNE SUPÉRIEURE RIEN
A LA GRACE QUI NE S'ABSENTE JAMAIS A LA NATURE

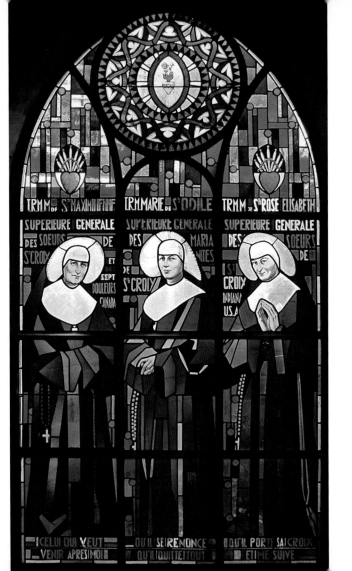

TRM M DE S.MAXIMILIENNE • TRM MARIE DE S.ODILE • TRM M DE S.ROSE ELISABETH

SUPÉRIEURE GÉNÉRALE
DES SOEURS DE
S.CROIX
ET
DE
SEPT
DOULEURS
CANADA

SUPÉRIEURE GÉNÉRALE
DES MARIA
NITES
DE
S.CROIX

SUPÉRIEURE GÉNÉRALE
DES SOEURS
DE
CROIX
INDIANA
U.S.A

CELUI QUI VEUT • QU'IL SE RENONCE • QU'IL PORTE SA CROIX
VENIR APRÈS MOI • QU'IL QUITTE TOUT • ET ME SUIVE

TRP A.COUSINEAU   Mgr G.GRENTE   TRP J.DONAHUE

SUPERIEUR GENERAL   ARCHE   SUPERIEUR GENERAL
DE LA   VEQUE   DU   DE LA   CONGREGATION
CONGRE   GATION   MANS   DE Ste CROIX
DE SAINTE   CROIX   RP.GAGNON
       CSC.CURE
       FONDATEUR

VITRAUX-ART
E.RAULT.RENNES

TRANSLATION DU CORPS   CONSECRATION DE L'EGLISE 1933   RETOUR AU BERCEAU
DU PERE MOREAU 1938   ERECTION DE LA PAROISSE 1933   DE LA CONGREGATION 1931

Vos Constitutions et vos Règles étant l'expression certaine de la volonté de Dieu sur vous, et le moyen assuré de votre Sanctification, attachez-vous y, méditez-les, pratiquez-les, et tous les jours votre ange gardien tracera la couronne qui vous attend au Ciel.

B. Moreau

Bas-relief found in the church of Notre-Dame-de-Sainte-Croix. From the beginning, Basile Moreau placed his religious family under the patronage of the Holy Family.

Basile Moreau – A Precursor

Notre-Dame de Sainte-Croix will grow like a mighty tree and constantly shoot forth new limbs and branches, which will be nourished by the same life-giving sap. (*Circular Letter*, June 15, 1854)

When Father Moreau wrote these prophetic lines, the little seed sown in the soil of Le Mans had grown into a tree whose branches were already spreading out to the four continents.

A tree: the customary way of representing a family, with its roots descending into the more or less distant past and whose new generations are the branches.

A tree: the symbol of organic unity, like the body; we know how much the Founder of Holy Cross insisted on a spirit of union within his religious family.

A tree: the symbol of dynamic unity: the family of Holy Cross was not trapped in the past; it was expected to develop according to the wishes of its Founder, who, although a man of his time, was nonetheless a precursor.

Basile Moreau was a precursor when he founded a congregation unlike any other of its time. He called upon clerical religious and lay religious to work together on an equal footing, and even added a society of religious women to the association. From this singular association, there followed that spirit of union and brotherhood which was to be the distinctive feature of the Holy Cross family. Among the sisters, brothers, and priests, as in any family, spontaneous ties of sincere esteem and cordial affection were supposed to grow.

> Notwithstanding differences of temperament and talent, the inequality of means, and the differences of vocation and obedience, the one aim of the glory of God and the salvation of souls ... gives rise to a oneness in effort which tends toward that more perfect union of hearts which constitutes its bond and strength. (*Circular Letter* September 1, 1841)

He was a precursor also in the way he planned the government of his congregation. At a time when centralized forms of power were yielding to more democratic ways in civil society, in the church it was quite the opposite, and centralization became more and more widespread. Father Moreau, however, purposely provided collegial structures for his community. He gave the chapters at every level true decision making powers. His vision was truly that of a community that was "the work of everyone" and whose members "shared responsibility in solidarity." (*Circular Letter*, January 10, 1843)

Again, he was a precursor in his apostolic vision. Many of his contemporaries were involved in the task of renewing the Catholic Church, but only a few attempted as he did to respond to such a wide range of needs both in the Church and in society. He sent the first members of the congregation out into a diversity of apostolic fields and asked them all " ... to be ready to turn their hands to anything ... to bear with anything and to go anywhere obedience called to save souls and spread the kingdom of Jesus Christ on earth." (*Rule on Zeal*)

Father Moreau was indeed a precursor. His projects were too audacious for his times. To obtain pontifical approval he was obliged to cut them back, to modify them. However, his original vision remained a dream for the future. The spirit of union, neglected for a long time, remained an ideal. Eventually, one day the four Holy Cross congregations would weave new ties of brotherhood and cordial affection. Together in beautiful unanimity, they requested that the Church consider the cause of beatification of their Founder. Encouraged by the Second Vatican Council's appeal for a renewal of religious life, they endeavoured to draw closer to his original design: "In accordance with the bold spirit of their Founder," they expressed the wish to "create new ways of being present amongst men and new forms of apostolate which would better respond to the urgent requirements of the Church." Religious men and women of Holy Cross began to draw more on the teachings of Father Moreau and to follow the example he set in his life.

In the Bible, the tree, strong and full of vitality, was the symbol of the just man who is blessed by God: "Like a tree planted in the garden of my God shall the just person flourish," sings the psalmist. This image fits Basile Moreau very well: he is the just man who lived a life of faith, the just man persecuted in the name of justice, the just man whom the Church is about to declare "blessed"! He himself, however, applied that image to every member of Holy Cross.

> You are a tree planted in the garden of the Church. Now a tree is known by the fruit it bears, and if the sap of grace flows in the veins of this living tree, its branches must bring forth first leaves, then buds, followed by flowers and lastly fruits of an extraordinary flavor. (*Christian Meditations*, p. 23)

> Everyone is called to holiness. The main purpose of the congregation is the "perfection" of its members "through the practice of the evangelical counsels." (*Constitutions*, 1857)

For almost 200 years, thousands of men and women have allowed themselves to be guided down the paths of holiness by Basile Moreau. Two members of the religious family of Holy Cross have already been proclaimed blessed: Brother André, founder of the St. Joseph Oratory in Montreal, and Mother Marie-Léonie Paradis, foundress of the Little Sisters of the Holy Family. The beatification of the Founder of the Congregation of Holy Cross will encourage the men and women of the 21st century to live their faith far better "in the pursuit of Jesus Christ."

The body of Basile Moreau has been in the crypt of the church of Notre-Dame-de-Sainte-Croix since November 29, 1938. The recumbent statue is the work of sculptor Henri Charlier. It was placed there on July 21, 1955 ,on the occasion of the introduction of the Cause of beatification of the Founder of Holy Cross.

II

DECREES OF THE CONGREGATION FOR THE CAUSES OF SAINTS RELATIVE TO BASILE MOREAU

BASILE-ANTOINE MARIE MOREAU

Priest and Founder of
The Congregation of Religious Men and Women of Holy Cross
(1799 – 1873)

DECRETUM SUPER VIRTUTIBUS

"Behold, God is my salvation; I will trust and will not be afraid" (Is. 12:2)

The servant of God, Basile Antoine Marie Moreau, with no confidence in merely human means, placed his trust in God and found in Him the strength to face countless difficulties and overcame severe hardship. In the aftermath of the French Revolution, he effectively devoted himself to the spiritual renewal of the Church through parish missions, the Christian education of youth, and various other works of charity. In order to ensure the stability and the continuity of his works, he founded a new religious family with two branches, one for men, the other for women, known as the Congregation of Holy Cross.

This true witness to Christ was born on February 11, 1799, in the village of Laigné-en-Belin (Sarthe, France), to a family of merchants. He was taught Christian morals by his family and the catechism by his parish priest, who also taught him the basics of literature. He entered the local College of Château-Gontier and later, the Seminary at Le Mans, where he studied philosophy and theology.

He was ordained a priest on August 12, 1821, and, in order to continue his training, he was sent by his bishop to the Seminary of Saint-Sulpice in Paris, where he devoted himself to further study for two years. On his return to Le Mans, he assumed his responsibilities for teaching philosophy, dogmatic theology, and Sacred Scripture. At the same time, he was constantly involved with additional pastoral activities. Deeply concerned with the Kingdom of God and the salvation of souls, he established a society of diocesan priests in August, 1835, to help pastors, especially in rural areas, in their ministry of preaching. Shortly after this, he received a mandate from his bishop to care for the Institute of the Brothers of Saint Joseph, which had been established fifteen years earlier by Father Jacques-François Dujarié, a priest from the same diocese. This Institute had been founded to provide for the primary education of boys living in the villages of the region. The Servant of God joined his society of priests with those of the Brothers of Saint Joseph, a union created by the so-called "Fundamental Act" of March 1, 1837. He thereby laid the foundation for the Congregation of Holy Cross, dedicated to assist the pastoral and educational needs of the Church in France, which had recently suffered great devastation. In 1838, the Servant of God gave a rule of life to a group of women he had gathered in order to assist the Priests and Brothers of Holy Cross. These women were given the tasks of housekeeping and caring for the sick in his educational institutions. Later, he entrusted them with the responsibilities of teaching. On August 15, 1840, the Servant of God was the first priest of the new Congregation of Holy Cross to publicly pronounce his religious vows. His religions priests, brothers, and sisters were known as "Salvatorists," "Josephites," and "Marianites" of Holy Cross. Later, at the request of the Holy See, the Sisters became a Congregation of Pontifical Right, under the name of the "Marianites of Holy Cross," which obtained the approval of the Holy See in 1867, whereas the men's Institute had already received papal approval in 1857.

The work founded by the Servant of God to spread the Gospel in rural regions and foreign missions, and to provide a Christian education for youth in need of material and spiritual assistance, developed rapidly, extending to North America and the American continent. The Founder also opened the first rural orphanage in Rome at the request of Blessed Pope Pius IX, who conferred on him the title of Apostolic Missionary. Yet, as often happons to the friends of God and to faithful witnesses of the Gospel, Father Basile was bound to undergo false accusations and rejection.

Indeed, some members of the Institute, to which he had completely dedicated himself, accused him unjustly of mismanagement, even alleging tyrannical control. For this reason, he thought it best to resign as Superior General. His decision was rejected by the Holy See at first, but was later accepted.

He endured these sufferings with remarkable serenity, finding consolation through his faith in Christ, who enlightened his path. He firmly believed in the truth of Revelation, and in his preaching, he constantly proclaimed these truths to the people of God. He nourished his own spirituality through the Eucharist and through his devotion to the Blessed Virgin Mary and to Saint Joseph. Throughout his lifetime, he kept his mind fixed on Heaven.

He lived in the sight of God and turned his thoughts and works towards Him. The love of Christ motivated him to become prolific in his apostolic activity and to undertake his work for the glory of God and the salvation of souls. Both by the example of his life and his writings, he made every effort to exhort others to avoid every kind of sin. A man of tireless activity, he accepted innumerable sacrifices for the good of others, in whom he beheld the face of the Divine Redeemer.

Some of the members of his Congregation, through negligence, were the cause of serious economic problems; yet, he acted with such a sense of prudence and justice that he protected both the good reputation of the Institute as well as the legitimate rights of its creditors. He was faithful to the laws of the Church and to the Rule of the Institute that he founded. He admirably mastered his somewhat impetuous nature. He led a simple and austere life, willingly adding acts of penance to those already prescribed by Church discipline. With patience and the deepest spirit of humility, he endured innumerable adversities and illnesses. During a time in which Gallicanism was rampant, he remained faithful to the Holy See. He persevered in following the advice of his spiritual director and was detached from material goods as well as being a model of chastity.

In the last years of his life, he continued his apostolic work as a substitute priest. He died in Le Mans on January 20, 1873. Before going to his eternal reward, he forgave all those who had caused him harm in any way.

With his reputation for sanctity spreading, the bishop of Le Mans started to work on his cause for beatification, initiating the information gathering stage between the years 1947-1950. Following the Decree for the Introduction of the Cause, dated May 2, 1955, the Apostolic Process was undertaken from 1955-1957. The Congregation of Rites, in a decree published October 23, 1959, recognized the legal validity of these canonical investigations. After the meeting of the

Historical Advisors, which occurred on December 6, 1994, the usual study was made to see if the Servant of God had practiced the virtues to an heroic degree. On January 31, 2003, the Special Meeting of the Theological Advisors gave a unanimous response to the question under study. The cardinals and bishops present at the ordinary session on March 18, 2003, after having heard the report of the Postulator for the Cause, His Excellency Émile Eids, Titular Bishop of Sarepta of the Maronites, declared that the Servant of God, Basile Antoine Marie Moreau, had practised the theological virtues, along with the related cardinal virtues, to an heroic degree.

After the presentation of the complete report by the undersigned Cardinal Prefect to the Sovereign Pontiff, John Paul II, His Holiness received the request of the Congregation for the Causes of Saints. He approved it and ordered the proclamation of the Decree on the heroic virtues of the Servant of God.

In the presence of the undersigned Cardinal Prefect, along with the Postulator of the Cause, and before me, the Secretary Archbishop of the Congregation and those duly convened, the Holy Father then solemnly declared: We declare that Father Basile Antoine Marie Moreau, Priest, Founder of the men and women religions of the Congregation of Holy Cross, practiced the theological virtues of Faith, Hope, and Love towards God and neighbor, as well as the related cardinal virtues of Prudence, Justice, Temperance, and fortitude, to an heroic degree.

The Sovereign Pontiff ordered that the Decree to this effect be made public and placed among the Acts of the Congregation for the Causes of Saints.

Given in Rome, in the year of Our Lord, April 12, 2003.

Joseph CARDINAL SARAIVA MARTINS, Prefect
Edouard NOWAK, Titular Archbishop of Luna, Secretary.

Le Mans
Beatification and Canonization of the Venerable Servant of God

BASILE-ANTOINE MARIE MOREAU
Priest and Founder of
The Congregation of Holy Cross
(1799 – 1873)

DECREE SUPER MIRACULO

The Venerable Servant of God, Basile-Antoine Marie Moreau, was born on February 11, 1799, in the town of Laigné-en-Belin. A priest of the diocese of Le Mans, France, he was a dedicated professor at the major seminary who devoted himself fully to his pastoral duties. He founded the Congregation of Holy Cross which is made up of three branches: Salvatorists (Priests), Josephites (Brothers), and Marianites (Sisters). After encountering many trials and tribulations during his life, on January 20, 1873, very piously breathed his last breath.

The Supreme Pontiff, John Paul II, declared on April 12, 2003, that the Servant of God had exercised the heroic practice of virtue.

For his beatification, the Postulation of the Cause submitted to this Congregation for its examination the alleged miraculously recovery of a Canadian woman named Laurette Comtois, who after giving birth to a prematurely deceased foetus on June 1, 1948, manifested symptoms of a dry cough, fever, and pain in the left hemi-thorax. After being diagnosed with pleuritis of the left lung, the sick woman was given the treatment appropriate for her case; yet, her condition worsened. On the 18th of that same month of June, a decision was taken to do a thoracentesis. In the meantime, the Sisters and the novices of the Congregation of Holy Cross, the patient, her father, and other people began invoking divine assistance through the intercession of the Servant of God, Basile-Antoine Marie Moreau. On the night between the 17th and 18th of the same month, the sick woman completely recovered her good health; the pleural fluid was quickly reabsorbed thus making the thoracentesis unnecessary, and her fever disappeared along with all other infections related to her illness. Thus, this woman was declared to have recovered faster than normal.

Concerning this recovery, which was judged to be miraculous, in 1950 the Archdiocese of Montreal carried out a canonical trial whose juridical validity was decreed by this dicastery on January 24, 2003. In their meeting on January 27, 2005, the Medical Consultants recognized that her recovery had been quick, perfect, lasting, and inexplicable from a scientific point of view. Having received this positive opinion, the meeting of the Theological Consultants was held on April 15 of the same year. The following November 8, during the meeting of the Ordinary Congregation and after having listened to the *Ponentis Causae*, His Most Reverend Excellency, Msgr. Lorenzo Chiarinelli, bishop of Viterbo, the Cardinal and Bishop Fathers asserted that Mrs. Laurette Comtois' recovery was truly miraculous.

Hence, the Cardinal Prefect, after having written up a careful report of all these events for the Supreme Pontiff, Benedict XVI, His Holiness gathered the opinions of the Congregation for the Causes of Saints, ratified them and on this day has declared:

It follows that the miracle performed by God through the intercession of the Venerable Servant of God, Basile-Antoine Marie Moreau, priest and founder of the Congregation of Holy Cross, i.e., that Mrs. Laurette Comtois' recovery from "pleuropneumonia with massive effusion in the left hemithorax in puerperium" was swift, perfect and lasting.

The Supreme Pontiff then decided that this decree should be made public and conserved among the acts of the Congregation for the Causes of Saints.

Given in Rome on April 28, in the year of the Lord 2006.

Joseph CARDINAL SARAIVA MARTINS, Prefect

Edward NOWAK, Secretary

III

CHARISM OF HOLY CROSS, SPIRITUALITY, MISSION AND COMMUNITY LIFE

A "charism" is a gift of the Spirit that is given individually or collectively for the common good and the building up of the Church. Inherent in this gift is a particular perception of the image of Jesus Christ and of the Gospel. It is, therefore, a source of inspiration, a dynamic commitment, and a capacity for realization.

The Charism of Holy Cross

Basile Moreau was a man open to the world of his time, namely 19th-century France. He knew the effects of the revolutionary change and social upheaval of his century. He also experienced the often violent hostility towards religion and the Church, the growth of secularism, and wide-spread dechristianization. He wanted to be present to a society in search of itself. He felt called to work for the restoration of the Christian faith and through it for a regeneration of society. He was ready to undertake anything for the salvation of individuals, to lead them or bring them back to Jesus Christ. He participated in the work of Catholic renewal by his bold response to the wide range of needs both in the Church and in society. He asked his religious to "be ready to undertake anything ... to suffer everything and to go wherever obedience calls in order to save souls and extend the kingdom of Jesus Christ on earth: (*Rule on Zeal*). He even went so far as to say that if a postulant or a novice did not have that inner zeal to work for the salvation of souls, he was not fit for Holy Cross. However, Father Moreau did not want to confine himself merely to post-revolutionary French society; he also wanted to devote himself to announcing the Gospel in other cultures. His zeal knew no borders.

The charism of Holy Cross is to renew the Christian faith, to regenerate society, to "bring about better times" by a constant response to the most pressing needs of the Church and society. The principal work that Basile Moreau advocated was education; he saw education as being explicitly a work of "resurrection," of rebuilding. In everything he undertook, he did not just want to re-establish it; he wanted to renew it, to refashion it, to reconstruct it. He had no fear of a brand new undertaking.

This charism, this mobilizing and efficacious strength of conviction, he drew from the perception of Jesus the savior, Jesus the liberator, and from the Gospel which leads humanity to fulfillment. "Once Jesus is known and loved in the world, everything will be renewed; the light of the Gospel will dissipate the darkness of the century; its morality will control customs and justice will reign" (*Sermons*, p. 455). A professor of Holy Scripture, Father Moreau arrived at a just and essential vision of the Gospel: the Good News of the Kingdom of God, the building up of the kingdom that is already coming, the rebuilding of a world according to God's heart.

The Congregation's charism is rooted in a spirituality; it is expressed in mission and inspires community life. It is therefore made up of three elements: spirituality, notably a particular grasp of the mystery of Jesus Christ; mission, that is, its apostolic focus; and community life, in this case a unique style of community. The spiritual and the apostolic direction received from the Founder is communicated to the members and influences the continuity and development of their works.

The Four Pillars of Holy Cross Spirituality

Conformity to Christ

The charism of the Congregation of Holy Cross is rooted in an experience of Jesus Christ. The founder's spirituality is fully centered on Jesus Christ, with access to his person notably in contemplation of the scriptures and the liturgy. Father Moreau believed that it is the essence of religious life to conform oneself to Christ, not only in his external conduct, but in his very being as a religious person. Father Moreau invites his religious to "re-enact the life of Jesus" and to make it "a faithful imitation": "Our spirit of discipline will imitate His habitual conformity to the good pleasure of His Father, while our community spirit will reflect His life in the company of Our Blessed Lady, St. Joseph and His apostles. Our life of edification will reproduce His life of good example in the midst of the world, and our spirit of work will mirror His labors and His cross." (CL 14). Father Moreau invites us to become "copies of the divine model" (CL 11).

Jesus serves especially as a model for us by his life, his words and his actions. He moved ceaselessly among people of all conditions of life, particularly among the poor, and he was compassionate towards every form of suffering. How are we to imitate him? "Our savior announced only the great and glad tidings which he had brought into the world, and spoke unceasingly of the Kingdom of God" (CL 36), and "We must seek above all things the kingdom of heaven and its justice" (CL 20).

Trust in Divine Providence
Jesus Christ, our model, is both the revelation of God's initiating love and the manifestation of human cooperation with it. Basile Moreau, convinced that Holy Cross is the work of God, demands of us "correspondence to the inspirations of grace and our fidelity in seconding the designs of Divine Providence" (CL 23). If we are to be faithful to this providential work of God in Holy Cross today, we must attend to God's constant presence and activity, for God himself gives us the desire to further his will in all things.

The Cross, Our Only Hope

Basile Moreau invites each religious person to carry his cross: "it is necessary to know the mystery of the cross and draw from it the apostolic strength of those generous imitators of Jesus Christ whose life here below was a continuous martyrdom" (CL 11). This invitation extends to courage in trials and demands that we "become more and more conformed to the image of the divine Christ crucified" (CL 34). Christ crucified, who gave his life for the salvation of the world, was so important to Father Moreau that he gave as a motto to his congregation: *The Cross, our only hope*, and proposed as the patronal feast of the entire congregation, *Our Lady of Seven Sorrows*, the title of Mary at the foot of the cross.

This cross is a glorious cross. It is the love of the suffering Savior expressed in the cross which is glorious, not the instrument of torture or of pain. Jesus' death takes all its meaning in the love with which he faithfully accomplished his mission in life, a love that goes to the end of its commitments. The cross is the source of salvation and liberation, and it is our hope.

Spirit of Union

Basile Moreau also insists on a union among the members in imitation of the union that existed in the Holy Family and in Jesus' relationship with his Father in fellowship with the Holy Spirit. This union is based on each individual's personal relationship with Jesus. Just as the members are organically connected to form a single body and as the branches are united with the vine and share the same life-giving sap, so also must the faithful of Holy Cross be united with Jesus and with one another.

Mission

The focal points proper to mission at the time of foundation were on the one hand, the evangelization of the dechristianized countryside for which Father Moreau formed a team of auxiliary priests and on the other hand, the education and Christian formation of youth confided first of all to the brothers. With the establishment of the Association of Holy Cross, Father Moreau provided a common mission, which was later expressed in the first constitutions of the priests and brothers as: "preaching the divine word in the countryside and in the foreign missions ... instruction and Christian formation of youth with a particular concern for poor and abandoned children." The mission of the sisters is to "instruct and raise youth in a Christian manner by establishing and directing, either in France or in its overseas colonies, not only elementary schools, but also boarding houses, sewing rooms, hostels, etc., especially for the poor and abandoned children."

The renewal of Catholic faith always involved the analysis of the needs of the Church and society, which, first of all, had to be discerned. The often bold response to these needs would lead to varied apostolic fields of endeavor. However, everything revolved around education, which Brother Moreau called a work of resurrection. We must be educators, witnesses showing the way to others. The common mission's point of cohesion is education, with a privileged position given to evangelization. This is a holistic education of individuals, preparing young generations to be responsible citizens and good laborers for earth and heaven, forming "men conformed to Jesus Christ" by education in the faith through activities of Christian formation and by putting in place pastoral activities based on local needs.

Our constitutions take up this focus of mission by identifying us as educators in the faith. Recent general chapters determined our mission priorities: proclaiming the Gospel as educators in the faith and the preferential option for the poor, a privileged means for proclaiming the Good News of the Kingdom of God.

Community Life

This charism of restoration for Christian renewal is also incarnated in community life. Institutional religious life, as a sign, seeks to anticipate the reconciliation, the collaboration and the communion desired by human beings. Basile Moreau was a pioneer when he founded a congregation that resembled no other of his time. He called together priests, brothers, and sisters of Holy Cross who were to live and work together on an equal footing. The spirit of union and fraternity was to be the mark of this association. The source of the Founder's concern that the union of hearts was to assure this unique style of community.

"Here, not withstanding differences of temperament and talent, the inequality of means, and differences of vocation and obedience, the one aim of the glory of God and the salvation of souls inspires almost all the members and gives rise to a oneness of effort which tends towards that more perfect union of hearts which constitutes its bond and strength" (CL 14).

Even today, despite the forced separation of the sisters' society from the congregation, the fact of being a religious family of three distinct societies united in equality is the most specific element in relation to other religious communities composed of several branches. Father Moreau endowed his foundation with a mystic intention: the union of hearts within the Holy Family of Nazareth is an example. The three societies would form a single family, the Family of Holy Cross: within these societies there would be established an effective collaboration in mission. His perspective was that of a community that was "the work of each and everyone and whose members are individually and collectively responsible for it" (CL 17).

Holy Cross men and women religious are called to live out this evangelical call to union and to be conscious that they are members, each and every one, in Jesus Christ, as the branches are to the vine. Wherever they may be, the lived union of hearts is at the center of their life in community, their efforts, and their mission. The world needs this union of hearts to show that hope lives and that another world is possible.

Common Values

To live faithfully in conformity to Christ, our life in Holy Cross must be marked by certain characteristics or common values that flow from our spirituality, mission and community life:

- *Trust in Divine Providence* that makes us dependent upon God in all things;
- *Union of hearts* that recognizes the presence of Christ within and among us;
- *Compassion* that shares, even as Jesus and Mary did, in the lives and sufferings of others;
- *Courage* that risks all for the kingdom of God;
- *Zeal* that sets our hearts on fire, the audacity to make all things new, to make Christ known and loved;
- *Competence* that marks every aspect of our ministry;
- *Promotion of justice* and concern for the poor;
- *Closeness* to the people we serve and to our lay collaborators;
- *Family spirit* that binds our minds and hearts, in joys and sorrows, so that people will "see how they love one another."

A Charism for Today

Father Moreau's firmly rooted life in the society and the Church of his time, and his determination to bring about a renewal capable of regenerating them, remain for us part of the heritage he bequeathed to us. This should spur us on to reaffirm our missionary thrust in places where we live and work. We must re-capture the charism of Holy Cross in our present-day context, which in many ways is similar to the one known by our Founder: the crisis of religion, the climate of dechristianization, the growth of religious indifference and agnosticism, and the spread of violence and injustice are an urgent call for meaningful interventions.

We are called to re-evangelize and present the Christian faith in a new way. We must restore its credibility in our cultures. We must find concrete ways to rebuild our societies.

The charism of Holy Cross is still contemporary and urgent: to renew the Christian faith, to regenerate society, to "bring about better times" by a constant response to the most pressing needs of the Church and society.

Congregation of Holy Cross International
Commission on Consecrated Life
Text adapted for this publication
Rome, August 11, 2006

IV

THE CONGREGATIONS OF THE FAMILY
OF HOLY CROSS TODAY

Congregation of Holy Cross
Priests and Brothers

Generalate in Rome

> You did not choose me,
> but I chose you to go and
> bear fruit, fruit that
> will last (*John* 15:16)

God has sent the Son and the Spirit to renew the face of the earth. We, religious priests and brothers of Holy Cross, are sent to participate in this mission of God, revealed most fully in the life, death and resurrection of Jesus. For us, mission in the image of Jesus is the proclamation of Truth and the outreach of Love, moving beyond expected boundaries toward those most in need, breaking down barriers of fear, privilege, and prejudice, inviting all into one family.

We go to our world, embodying the Good News of Jesus, not as independent individuals but together, as Church, and blessed by the internationality of our communion in Holy Cross. We respond to the Church's call for a new evangelization. To all whom we serve, from those who have never known Jesus to those who ignore or reject him, we offer *"the precious legacy of human and Christian values which have given meaning to (our) lives"* (John Paul II, 1999). The diverse cultures and contexts in which we find ourselves as Holy Cross religious today help us to be aware of the complex realities of the world we are called to serve and open our eyes to the many faces of Jesus and works of the Spirit around the globe. They also give us a special lens through which to see and understand how to effectively proclaim the Risen Jesus and his message of salvation in our times – as Lord of Reconciliation, Lord of Hope, Lord of Dialogue, Lord of Justice, and Lord of Creation.

Our constitutions present mission as border-crossing activity. From the time of our founding, we have understood our responses to the needs of the world and the Church as calling us to cross borders. There is a richness and joy to be experienced when we cross these borders with open and generous hearts. But the borders in our world that are barriers, dividing God's family in fear, misunderstanding, and distrust, remain many. They are, as our constitutions state, "of every sort" – cultural and racial, national, religious, socio-economic, ideological – and we have learned that crossing them requires both "the competence to see and the courage to act."

Whatever the context in which we find ourselves, the words of our founder, Basile Moreau, in his "Rule on Zeal," describe what is most basic: "If we have faith and the zeal that faith inspires, we will ... be ready to undertake anything ... to suffer anything and to go anywhere ... to save souls that are perishing and to extend the reign of Jesus Christ on earth."

At this time, when the globalization of market forces, technology, and culture is so pervasive, we desire to promote a commitment to the globalization of solidarity in the teaching, healing, and sanctifying mission of Jesus. We affirm two priorities for our mission as religious of Holy Cross: the preferential option for the poor, and the proclamation of the truth of the Gospel as educators in the faith. These two interrelated priorities are at the heart of our charism as Holy Cross and are to give direction to the border-crossing mission in each of our ministries. We are convinced that this mission effort in each local context will be enriched by attention to and connection with our Holy Cross life and mission in other contexts. Our diversity, shared in a spirit of mutuality, solidarity, and interdependence, is a valuable resource for mission and a gift we can offer to all whom we serve.

Hugh CLEARY, C.S.C.

Marianites of Holy Cross

Generalate in New-Orleans, Louisiana, USA

Basile Moreau was an organizer, but more than an organizer, he was a founder. He saw needs in the Church of his day which stemmed from the lack of priests, the lack of Christian educators, lack of assistance to the poor and the marginated of society. In 1838, Brother Moreau gave a rule of life to a group of women who were to assist the priests and brothers in the linen room and infirmary of his school which was attached to the mother house in the section of Le Mans known as Ste. Croix (Holy Cross). After a brief period of formation with the Good Shepherd religious of Le Mans, these women became the first Marianites of Holy Cross.

Under difficult circumstances, particularly the non-support of the diocesan bishops, Moreau succeeded in bringing the first Marianites through a period of basic religious formation. He accepted Leocadie Gascoin of

Montenay as one of his first religious women. She later received the name Mary of the Seven Dolors and became the first superior general of the Marianites.

Under the instruction and supervision of Mother Dositheus of the Good Shepherd religious, the first four Marianites made their vows on August 4, 1841. As their spiritual father, Basile Moreau received these women in the name of the Church and remained their respected father and Founder until his death.

Early on, Moreau's religious priests, brothers and sisters were known as Salvatorists, Josephites, and Marianites of Holy Cross. When the priests and brothers received papal approval on May 13, 1857, the Holy See insisted that the sisters become a distinct congregation of pontifical right. The Marianites were officially approved by Rome in 1867. Growth of the congregation was rapid and requests for religious, missions were answered by Brother Moreau. As much as possible, he sent priests, brothers, and sisters to Asia, Africa, and North America. On these missions, Brother Moreau allowed the Marianites to devote themselves to both education and care of the sick.

The early history of the Marianites of Holy Cross is filled with examples of fidelity to God's gifts exemplified in stories of devotion and dedication, courage, and commitment. When Brother Moreau was rejected by his sons in Holy Cross, the Marianites remained his devoted and faithful daughters, even bringing him meals in the small house he occupied with his sisters.

Moreau's educational establishment of Holy Cross in Le Mans was the beginning of the Marianites' ministry in French schools, an endeavor which flourished in towns and hamlets until the French laws of 1901 closed Catholic schools. In 1854, the city of Le Mans asked for sisters to visit the sick in their homes. Besides caring for ailing bodies, the sisters had the consolation of preparing many of the elderly to meet their God. Finding so many poor among their charges, the sisters did not hesitate to beg firewood, food, clothing, and money for the most destitute. Then, joining the priests and brothers at a school in Montjean, France, the sisters bore all privations with patience, offering their trials to God for the success of their new mission.

Sent to Indiana in 1843 and to Canada in 1847, the first Marianites to arrive in North America found a world very different from that which they had left behind: a wild and untamed land of woods and lakes, but America was not unlike France in the work to be done, and the sisters set about doing it. With courage and commitment, they continued their ancillary services, eventually entering the field of education. This was the beginning of what would later become the other two congregations of women in Holy Cross, in Indiana and in Canada.

In April of 1849, five brothers and three sisters arrived by river boat in Louisiana and immediately took charge of St. Mary's Orphan Boys' Asylum in downtown

New Orleans. This ministry continued under the direction of the Marianites for over 80 years, and cared for more than 9000 orphans.

Among the Marianite pioneers, Sr. Mary of the Five Wounds saw the need to educate young girls long before the advent of women's liberation, and it was she who in 1851 established the Industrial School for Orphan Girls. Mother Mary of the Desert Godeau arrived in Louisiana in 1852 and spent thirty years at St. Mary's with her orphan boys. At Mother Desert's diamond jubilee in 1907, the city newspaper referred to "the boys who from her ministering care have gone forth into larger fields, recruits to swell the ranks of the priesthood, medical, legal, and musical professions ... "

The work of Holy Cross flourished so much in New Orleans that Brother Moreau wrote, "As soon as we can form a novitiate in New Orleans, we will make Louisiana a province." The novitiate opened on June 24, 1855, with two novices and eight postulants to occupy it. On December 1, 1858, Sr. Mary of St. Alphonsus Rodriguez was installed as provincial of the Louisiana province.

Sr. Mary of Calvary, first superior in Louisiana, spent her early years in New Orleans foraging for food for the orphans and the sisters. She was befriended in her mission by Union General Benjamin Butler during the Civil War. The war was raging when the foundation was laid for Holy Angels Academy which was dedicated in 1865. As word of their work spread, the Marianites were invited to staff schools outside of New Orleans, and by 1950, they were educating more students in the Catholic schools of Louisiana than any other religious congregation. When Holy Angels closed its doors in 1992, it was the oldest existing Marianite establishment in North America.

Heeding the mandate of Vatican II, and in ongoing fidelity to their history and Father Moreau's gift to the Church, the Congregational Chapters of the Marianites have challenged all the members to respond to new and changing needs in the Church and in society. Today Marianites are found in offices on the diocesan level, in administrative positions in the field of education, in health care, pastoral care, social work, and at all levels of service to the Church in Bangladesh, Canada, France, and the United States.

During their 2001 Congregational Chapter, the Marianites of Holy Cross gathered in New Orleans, Louisiana and listened to God's heart speaking through their prayers, reflections, discussions, deliberations, and faith sharing. In this spirit, the following mission statement was adopted:

> United with Mary standing at the foot of the cross, we, Marianites of Holy Cross, are apostolic religious, women of prayer and compassion. Our mission, energized by our life in community, is to incarnate the love and compassion of Jesus Christ. Called to be a prophetic presence in an ever-changing world, we resolutely stand with those who are excluded.

The Mission Statement begins in Mary's name to remind us of the woman whose name we bear and in whose name we were founded as a religious congregation. Father Moreau placed us under the special protection and guidance of Mary, Our Lady of Seven Dolors.

Union and unity are two of the words most frequently used by Brother Moreau in his circular letters. He was insistent that we not only speak about union, but that we live it in our lives. Our Founder envisioned the Marianites as women working, constructing, building union and communion wherever we are and with whomever we are associated. Inspired by his words in *Circular Letter # 14*, "Unity is the powerful lever with which to transform and sanctify the whole world," our Vision Statement reads:

> Faithful to the vision of unity which inspired our founder, Brother Basile Moreau, we, Marianites of Holy Cross, strive to be artisans of communion participating in the transformation of the Church and the world.

Today we are some 200 Marianites, 143 in the United States, 58 in France, and 10 in Canada. Blessed with capable and zealous younger sisters, we keep great hope for our future and believe what Pope John Paul II wrote in Vita *Consecrata 110*:

"You have not only a glorious history to remember and to recount, but also a great history still to be accomplished! Look to the future, where the Spirit is sending you."

Sr. Madeleine Sophie HEBERT, MSC
Sr. Mary Kay VIELLION, MSC

Sisters of the Holy Cross

Generalate in Notre Dame, Indiana, USA

The Sisters of the Holy Cross today are women who seek an ever-deepening relationship with God through prayer, community, compassionate service, and work for justice. Although our specific ministries have changed over the years, our mission has remained constant: We are called to participate in the prophetic mission of Jesus to witness God's love for all creation.

Our lives and spirituality are deeply rooted in world reality and in the gospel of Jesus. We stand in solidarity with the poor and the powerless to reflect on the signs of the times, discern needs, and respond. We are bound together, seeking strength and support from each other, through our shared dedication to this ongoing work.

Inspired by the vision and spirit of our founder, Basile Anthony Mary Moreau, and the sisters he sent to America in 1843, members today strive to confront contemporary problems and issues with compassion and justice. Our life together in community and our prayer together in ritual and liturgy enable us to live contemplatively in the present while we draw strength for action from our heritage. We continue to respond to the various needs of the world through a diversity of ministries in collaboration with many others. It is our conviction that by our united actions we can make a difference.

From our beginnings near Notre Dame, Indiana, we have grown to an international congregation with sisters ministering on the four continents of Asia, Africa, and North and South America. Our internationality enables us to better understand issues of poverty, ignorance, oppression, and injustice worldwide and address these issues systemically from a global perspective. As a congregation, we have taken corporate stands on a number of issues, including the oppression of women, the human right to water and to land, and nonviolence.

Our corporate stand on the oppression of women in social and religious structures calls us to work to eliminate the domination and subordination of women in society, the church, our ministries, our sponsored institutions, and our life together.

We realize that the violation of women's human rights is only one experience of violence in our life together on this planet. Our corporate stand on nonviolence calls us to reject violence in all its forms. We affirm nonviolence as a constitutive element of the message of Jesus, as we seek innovative, proactive ways to resist oppression and work to create right relationships with all of creation.

The mission of Jesus, Moreau's message, continues to be heard around the world. Our spirituality today leads us to seek interconnectedness as God's design for all, to maintain a stance of nonviolence, to revere the earth and walk the path of justice. In a global reality marked by dualities, we strive to live and worship in such a way that our prayer and our actions praise God, reverence the earth, contribute to beauty around us, and embody, as Father Moreau said, "that union which moves, directs, and sanctifies the world." Today, young women from various ethnic and cultural backgrounds throughout the world are joining with us to live that mission. As one of our newer members said so well, "We are one in Spirit. We belong to one family, even though we are different as persons, in language, culture, and country. We have one identity. We are Holy Cross sisters."

Frances B. O'CONNOR, c.s.c.

Sisters of Holy Cross

Generalate in Saint-Laurent, Quebec, Canada

The Canadian branch of the Sisters of Holy Cross, descendants of the Marianites of Holy Cross, reached St. Laurent in 1847. It quickly spread both to the north and south of the little village of St. Laurent.

As vocations arrived at Holy Cross, the requests for teachers became increasingly numerous. Québec undoubtedly contributed much to the expansion of the young community, as did the rest of Canada – Ontario, Alberta, Saskatchewan, Manitoba, British Columbia, and New Brunswick. Holy Cross was also very much in demand to open schools in New England (USA), where many families had immigrated from Québec. The "mission territories," as they were then called, enabled quite a number of sisters to practise their zeal, first in Bengal (now Bangladesh) and Haiti. There followed Africa (Cameroon, Rwanda, Burundi, and, more recently, Mali and Burkina-Faso). After that came Latin America (Peru, Chile, Costa Rica).

What is the situation today? In a world that changes constantly, Holy Cross has to adapt to many settings that do not necessarily require the kinds of traditional commitments typical of its original settlement in North American territory. We therefore need to distinguish between situations in North America and those in developing countries.

North America

In places where Holy Cross began in Canada and in the United States, the Congregation fulfilled a leading role in education. Faithful to its mission, the Congregation opened elementary and secondary schools, a few Colleges and Teachers' Training Colleges. Everywhere it offered students a wholistic education, involving the training of mind, heart, and the whole person. This mission so desired by Father Moreau was often able to supply that which the State could not:

> "Turn your hand to this task of resurrection, never forgetting that the special purpose of your institute is, above all, to sanctify the young. That is how you will contribute to preparing better times than ours for the world." (*Pedagogy*, p. 144)

After World War II, the technological revolution, amongst other changes, made it possible for modern society to take over, in an effective way, a task that had until then been the responsibility of religious congregations. Holy Cross escaped neither this movement towards secularization nor the crisis of vocations that marked the period following Vatican Council II.

The aging of the sisters, the small number of vocations to Holy Cross, and the new situation regarding teaching, in both Canadian and American schools, obliged the sisters to adapt their services. While a small number of sisters still teach in the formal educational system, others continue by tutoring once they have reached retirement age. Yet others have chosen to move to fields of apostolate where there is a shortage of "evangelical workers":

- faith education – children, youth, and adults in different situations
- pastoral care in the parish – when schools became non-denominational
- social pastoral care – in hospitals and prisons, social reinsertion, retreat and spiritual centres
- spiritual and psychological counselling
- commitment in major social issues
- involvement in poorer neighbourhoods, in cooperation with lay groups
- helping women, especially single mothers
- helping of the marginalized
- etc.

In many of these sectors, our sisters, together with the help of lay people and other communities, have undertaken a number of initiatives. For example, they have opened the Maisonnette for Parents, D-Trois-Pierres, and nature parks, The

Family Centre, The Pasto-Club, Cap-Vie, Berakah, Every Day Blessing, housing cooperatives, etc.)

Developing Countries

Parallel to this "apostolic reinsertion" movement, the Congregation has heeded the cry of the young Churches and in certain instances strengthened its missionary presence (in Haiti, for example), or opened up more mission areas in Africa (Mali, Burkina Faso) and in Latin America (Peru, Chile). Some major Holy Cross undertakings have seen the light of day. In Haiti, for example:

- Regina Assumpta College in Cap-Haitien has added a Faculty of Educational Sciences and a primary school in the last ten years;
- five other primary schools situated in different villages in the country have now extended their services to providing secondary schooling, or hope to do so in cooperation with the local people;
- the Hospital L'Espérance in Pilate offers quality care and has thus become a point of reference in this impoverished country.

In Mali, we have a Home Centre in Sikasso where high school or university students can stay and receive tutoring. This is greatly appreciated.

Wherever we have settled in Third World countries, our sisters are involved in different pastoral and social activities that support the local people in their endeavours to improve their lot both individually as well as collectively:

- teaching
- literacy
- hospital care
- educating young people and adults in the faith
- pastoral care in the parish
- vocation promotion
- empowering grassroots groups
- etc.

At the present time, several of our Third World members participate in the leadership of the Congregation on the regional and general levels. Some of our younger sisters are studying and preparing to respond to needs as numerous as they are urgent. The sisters who came from Canada and the United States are "holding the fort" until such time as they can take over a greater share of the Holy Cross mission, in their own country or elsewhere.

Holy Cross is experiencing a period of fragility and questioning at the moment, which is prompting it to deepen its faith in a God that continues to call whom He wills and where He wills. As Father Basile Moreau invited us:

> "Pray to the Lord of the harvest to send labourers into his harvest ... Try to bring vocations from wherever Providence has carried the work of Notre-Dame de Sainte-Croix." (*Circular Letter* 42)

Nevertheless, this fragility and questioning do not make us despair of the future. *The great tree of Holy Cross* has not completed its mission. Together with our Sister Graziella Lalande, we are convinced that "Holy Cross is still in genesis." Its present and its future are in our hands. God is still sending us out into the world today to do great and beautiful things, so long as we remain "in the Spirit to be reborn and risk" (General Chapter 2005).

Rollande BASTIEN, C.S.C.

In 2007, the Congregations of Holy Cross are present in the following countries

1. **Congregation of Holy Cross: Priests and Brothers**
1500 religious present in 15 countries
Bangladesh, Brazil, Canada, Chile, France, Ghana, Haïti, India,
Italy, Kenya, Mexico, Peru, Tanzania, Uganda, United States.

2. **Marianites of Holy Cross**
200 religious present in 4 countries
Bangladesh, Canada, France, United States

3. **Sisters of the Holy Cross (Indiana)**
500 religious present in 8 countries
Bangladesh, Brazil, Ghana, India, Peru, Tanzania,
Uganda, United States

4. **Sisters of Holy Cross (Canada)**
750 present in 10 countries
Bangladesh, Burkina Faso, Canada, Chile, Costa Rica,
Haïti, Italy, Mali, Peru, United States

V

CHRONOLOGY

P. Jean Proust, c.s.c

1799	February 11: Birth of Basile Moreau in Laigné-en-Belin
1814-17	Attends the school at Château-Gontier
1817-21	Attends the seminary in Le Mans
1820	In Ruillé, Father Dujarié establishes the Brothers of St Joseph
1821	August 12: Basile Moreau is ordained priest
1821-23	Further theological and spiritual studies with the Sulpicians
1823-36	Teaches at the seminary in Le Mans and preaches in the diocese
1833	Foundation of the Good Shepherd Monastery in Le Mans
1835	Foundation of the Auxiliary Priests and assumes direction of the Brothers of St Joseph
1836	Priests and brothers are regrouped at Holy Cross
1837	March 1: Act of Union between the priests and brothers
1838	First sisters at Holy Cross
1840	Foundation in Algeria
	August 15: Father Moreau makes his religious profession
	August 22: the Association of Holy Cross is born
	October 18: Blessing of the novitiate for the priests at La Solitude
1841	August 4th: Sister Mary of the Seven Dolors received the habit of the Marianites
	Foundation in the United States of America
1843	Marianite Sisters are sent to the United States
1844	September 15: Sister Mary of the Seven Dolors makes her religious profession
1847	Foundation in Canada: Priests, Brothers and Sisters
1849	Father Moreau is elected superior general for life
1850	Foundation in Rome

1853	Mission in Eastern Bengal
1855	October: Father Moreau's "night of the spirit"
1856	Foundation in Paris. Foundation in Poland.
1857	May 13: Approval by Rome of the Congregation of Holy Cross
	June 17: Consecration of the church of Notre-Dame de Sainte-Croix in Le Mans
	July – August: Father Moreau visits the foundations in America
1858	Father Moreau resigns as canon and superior of the Good Shepherd Community
1860	Father Moreau offers his resignation as superior general
1866	Pope Pius IX accepts Father Moreau's resignation
	Father Moreau resumes his ministry of preaching
1867	February 18: Approbation of the Congregation of Marianite Sisters
1868	General Chapter in Rome (St Brigid's); decision to sell the Mother House
1869	Father Moreau moves to live with his sisters on rue Jeanne D'Arc
	The Sisters of the Holy Cross in Indiana become autonomous
1872	August 17: Father Moreau's golden jubilee of ordination
1873	January 20: Father Moreau dies
	Burial in the community cemetery
1883	The Sisters of Holy Cross in Canada become autonomous
1900	January 29: Mother Mary of the Seven Dolors dies
1924	January 12: Exhumation of Father Moreau's remains and transfer to the cemetery chapel
1937	November 9: Second consecration of the Church of Notre-Dame de Sainte-Croix
1938	November 9: Transfer of Father Moreau's remains in the crypt of Notre-Dame de Sainte-Croix

1946	June: The superiors general of the four congregations of Holy Cross ask the bishop of Le Mans to introduce the cause of beatification of Father Moreau
1948	May 1: Opening of the informative process for beatification in Le Mans
1955	March 15: Opening of the apostolic process for beatification in Rome
	July 19: Recognition of the remains of Father Moreau
1974	Resumption of the cause for beatification following the historical documents
1982	May 23: Beatification of Brother André (Alfred Bessette)
1984	September 11: Beatification of Mother Mary Leonie (Alodie Paradis)
2003	April 12: Pope John Paul II declares Father Moreau Venerable
2006	April 28: Pope Benedict XVI announces the Beatification of Basile Moreau

TABLE OF CONTENTS